BUS RIDE TO A BLUE MOVIE

ALSO BY ANNE-MARIE LEVINE

Euphorbia

ANNE-MARIE LEVINE

Bus Ride to a Blue Movie

Pearl
Editions

LONG BEACH, CALIFORNIA

Grateful acknowledgment is made to the editors of the following journals where some of these poems first appeared:

American Letters and Commentary, CROSSCONNECT, *Gargoyle, Parnassus, Poetry Now, Provincetown Arts, Salamander, Tin House.* "Night's Bodies" appeared in *Euphorbia* (Provincetown Arts Press, 1994); "With Sophie" was published as a limited edition chapbook by Pea Pod Press (1999); and "Four November 9ths" appeared in *Poetry After 9/11: An Anthology of New York Poets* (Melville House Publishing, 2002).

Library of Congress Control Number: 2002110042

First edition

ISBN 1-888219-22-X

Book design by Marilyn Johnson

PEARL EDITIONS
3030 E. Second Street
Long Beach, California 90803
U.S.A.

CONTENTS

IV

BUS RIDE TO A BLUE MOVIE

I

RECENT RESEARCH REVEALS

Men who eat chocolate
live longer than those who don't.

Harvard men with post-
traumatic stress disorder
appear much more often

in *Who's Who* than their
less traumatized peers. In all
countries, the world over,

Women live longer,
regardless of health care de-
livery systems.

God eats the details.

NIGHT'S BODIES

"I sleep to escape my life,
arise to still my dreams . . . ."

❖

I am suffering from amusia,
the inability to produce musical sounds,
the loss of ability to make music.
The condition is desperate,
potentially fatal,
I know.

❖

I travel to France
to have the left hand joined
to the right at the wrist.
Surgery is required
to reinforce GROWTH and stability.
But the surgeons understand
BROKEN stability
and refuse to perform the operation.

❖

What do I know about trills?
  that they should be practiced slowly
  and played evenly   sometimes
  it helps to accent the first note
  or to start slowly and then speed up

          . . . practicing trivializes

❖

A friend confides that he is unable to quiet his inner voices.
I advise him never to lift his thumbs from the keys,
to press down on the note itself,
instead of striking from above.

❖

She lies, Noh-painted, between us
   We are helping her to die
   I am kind, but I cringe
when she touches me
She is a vision, white-masked, of myself
He says we are killing her
   She will no longer come between us
   "But I am kind!" I cry
You are, he says   Always

❖

The telephone rings in the middle of the night.
I am frightened out of deep sleep.
An unknown man's voice asks if I am Anne-Marie.
"Do you put polish on your toenails?" he asks
"What?" I gasp   "Do you?" he purrs

I dream that my legs are encased in primeval slime.
I am Anne-Marie.

GENIUS

She is a few feet off the ground,
fleeing.
She is running away from a man,
her cousin,
down a road that is covered
with white debris,
paper and fluff.
She is using not her legs
but her arms
in a sort of flapping
flying
and at the same time swimming
motion.
"Are you a genius?"
he yells.
She thinks it may satisfy him
if she answers
even while running,
so she yells "No!"
But he continues to chase her
and she continues to flee.
"You belong to the tribe of Michel!"
he screams.
Michel is his father,
her father's brother.
She keeps running.
She begins to tire —
the arm motions,
the wing-flapping.
She falls exhausted into the road.
She sinks into the white stuff
that covers the road,
and she sinks beneath it
as he approaches
so that she too is covered,
hidden. He passes over her.
She is saved.

You Won't Like This Poem

He told me I didn't know enough.
I thought he was probably right.
I wanted to compose as well as play concerts,
to study with John Cage . . .
But my coach said no,
you can't do that, you don't know enough yet.

I worked hard at the piano.
I tried to understand Beethoven,
to learn his thirty-two piano sonatas,
and to improve my technique.
But I was distracted.

I began to write poems.
My boyfriend said, "If you become a poet
as well, I'll kill you."
By spring I had stopped
composing and writing poems
and playing in public.

I tried to do what they expected,
what they said they wanted:
cook eggs for breakfast,
practice the piano.

I thought they wanted me
to learn more, to be a better pianist.
I didn't know they wanted me
to be still.

Since then
I've been a pianist
and I am still . . .
I've been a poet
and I am still . . .

You won't like this poem.

But this spring I composed.
I wrote a flute solo for my son.
He wanted me to compose it.
But he can't play it.
He doesn't know enough.

Solo for David

DREAMS, FRAGMENTS

A baby lies in a man's hand
It does not breathe
We try hard to revive it
I jump up and down
We fail
I cry and cry

The baby is mine
It is I
We are the baby
It is the aborted twin

The hand is yours

"I can't go on, I'll go on"

I make an appointment to have my vocal cords cut

"Everyone possesses in his own unconscious an instrument
with which he can interpret the utterances of the unconscious
in another"

There is a record in the body of what happened

Memory muscles out invention

May one loose one's Holocaust memories on another,
or must one keep them oneself?

If you had been clear-headed we could have gone farther

If you had been clear-headed I could have stayed longer

"You are my son. Your book will be the child of my book."

POEMS

Something unnameable is laming me.
—Paul Celan

In a book on rare diseases in the medical library
while researching myopathies like MAD
(myo-adenylate de-aminase de-ficiency)
in which exercise can trigger muscle fatigue
and weakness in your limbs, so that you would be
unable to achieve previous performance levels
— meaning that pianists might not be able to play
(amusia) or poets to write (hypographia) —

I discover, in my confusion having missed "M"
and come across "P," a disorder called POEMS.
It is an even more sinister constellation
of anomalies: [P]olyneuropathy causes tingling,
numbness, burning pain, deficiencies in perception,
and vibratory sensations in the limbs; [O]rgan-
omegaly sounds as though it would cause vibratory
sensations, but instead causes abnormal enlargement
of the liver and spleen; [E]ndocrinopathy would
affect your sexual functioning and your thyroid;
[M] is for elevated serum levels of M and other
abnormal proteins; your [S]kin would be thick
and hyperpigmented. There you have POEMS.
There are other symptoms and signs
and even treatments, standard and investigational,
but they don't fit the acronym.

It is a perfectly terrible disease
and we don't like terrible diseases,
as Frank O'Hara said when asked by a lady
for a contribution — "we don't give her one
we don't like terrible diseases"

But this disease is called POEMS
and I do like it, it seems sort of wonderful
and so literary too — there is even a list of synonyms
for it — or is it the book that is very literary to give
us these synonyms — and they are wonderful too —
PEP syndrome and Shimpo, Takatsuki syndrome
and Crow-Fukase.

Why is this so wonderful, why am I so happy?
(They don't give her a contribution)
It is a terrible disease,
not like the one I am looking up
whose acronym is MAD but which is mysterious,
invisible, untreatable, barely believable
even to those who suffer from it as pianists
and poets, athletes or even a doctor, my friend,
whose own physicians tell her she's "de-
conditioned" and to get herself a personal trainer.
(They don't give *her* a contribution either)
"Cheryl," they say, "you can't have this disease,
it's too rare."

The question I'm asking myself is what does it mean
for a poet with a too rare disorder called MAD
to come across a rare enough disorder called POEMS

in a book? Of course they are only acronyms,
it is only a coincidence. But what are coincidences
but the visible traces of untraceable principles,
as the physicist said. But what principles?
Is there a connection between MAD and POEMS,
between names and disease?   Is there meaning in this
MADness?   Can you make poems out of disease?
Finding a disorder called POEMS in a book is good medicine
There is joy in acronyms

There is joy in O'Hara's poem, "but now I'm happy
for a time and interested," he says, "happy at the
thought possibly so"

Is happiness contagious   I think I have caught it

Tunnel Vision

What, in your own words, are you here for?
(questionnaire in the 48th Street MRI office).
In your own words, what are your symptoms?
When was your last period?

Transvaginal sonogram, I wrote.
Jupiter, planet of growth, is passing through
my 6th House. Exuberant growths sometimes appear
under this aspect. My menopausal energy is occurring.

The technician was brusque
and inserted an icy stainless steel pear,
transvaginally.
She moved it around while peering at the monitor.
Her concentration was complete.
How are you? she asked presently.
Do you want to say something?

As a matter of fact, I replied,
I do have something to say.
If you're ever on a quiz show
and they ask you,
how long does it take for a vagina
to warm up an ice cold transducer,
I've been thinking about it —
the answer is five minutes.
Yeah that's good, if they ever ask me,
she cackled.

The doctor entered.
How are you? he asked.
Jesus.
He sat down.
I won't be long, he said,
moving the transducer around,
studying the monitor.

And then, as I moved my knees
ever so slightly
to relieve muscle tension,
Don't kick me, he said.
(Don't kick me?)
I was flabbergasted.
Do women kick you? I asked.

I thought you might want to get even, he said.
I began to imagine the inside of his head,
no sonogram or MRI necessary.
His fantasy, or maybe his reality,
that he was transgressing (with a transducer)
and might be, or better yet deserved to be
punished, attacked . . .

I, on the other hand, hadn't even realized
I had a weapon.
I'm not aggressive enough by half.
I don't think like an adversary.
It's true, I was perfectly positioned
to give him a swift kick in the face or the chest.
Nothing to it, and I hadn't even thought of it.

There's always a lot to be learned.

And then he stopped.
You have a fibroid, he said, and a small cyst.
Your endometrium's thin,
just the way we like it.
Garden variety stuff.

Pumpkins and squash, I thought,
growing in my uterine cavity.
"A field of Ceres, ripe for harvest."
I felt like a fucking goddess.

It wouldn't be long till Thanksgiving.

II

MOURNFUL NUTRIENTS

Is semen safe to swallow?
Yes, it is sterile, it carries no germs.
But, according to a scientific study,
if a man has AIDS or other sexually
transmissible infections,
his semen may be harmful to swallow.

The AIDS virus appears in the semen of infected men
only 20% of the time, so you could gamble
if you like that sort of thing,
swallowing, or gambling . . .

However in men with none of these diseases
semen is safe to swallow.

You wouldn't catch cold . . .

But wait, there's more.
The authors say semen has calories.
You could gain weight.
On the other hand, they say it has
no nutritional value.
None? Like empty calories?
Right. Because semen is fully broken down
by gastrointestinal enzymes,
and then almost completely excreted
in body wastes.

Almost?

In details lie truth, rightness, splendor.

PORTRAIT OF AN INTELLECTUAL

Why do you want me so much? asked the waitress.
Because you're always 3000 miles away and because somebody else has you.
She dropped the crabs she was carrying.
Is he a good lover?
The best.
I don't want to hear any more. I'm sleeping on the couch.
Why did you ask?

The neurosis is not the man, he shouted, tearing his clothes off as he
ran through the girls' dorm,
was asked to resign;
advertised in *The New York Review of Books* for a woman,
found one,
came in her mouth without polite notice,
passed on the waitress' crabs.

OUT OF A STAMP ROLL AND 400 EGGS

You ask about my day
The day begins with news   radio news
of a sex fair and a new bacterium

Then Oprah presents a guest who says
that men produce 100 million sperm
every day   and women have only 400 eggs
to last a lifetime.   He explains
that a man can discover
if his impotence is psychological
or physical
          by
pasting a roll of stamps around his
      penis
while he sleeps.   It seems that
normal men
have several erections a night in their sleep
         so
if he wakes
to find the stamp roll broken apart
he knows he's capable of erection
  and the problem is psychological
not physical

At Macy's Department Store I stare
  but no one else does
at a gentleman shopping for shirts
He is properly dressed in a shirt-and-tie-and-jacket
  no pants

My mind begins to wander:

A former lover's face appears as a hot-dog vendor's
There is a sign on the hot-dog stand
  ALL BEEF, NO PEOPLE
We are not allowed to eat our lovers
But what of people we love?   Are we allowed
to eat them?   I think about that
Cronus and his children
Dali   *"de la beauté terrifiante et comestible"*
    edible beauty   may we eat beauty?
edible love   have we not all hidden
our pomegranates under the bed?

Out of a stamp roll and 400 eggs . . .
I wonder where the 100 million sperm go each day,
the ones that aren't used
if the stamp roll doesn't break

This is hard, you are
Hard.

On Being Clean

*For Teibele to be asked, as a matter of course
(before making love to a demon), whether she is
clean is, even in its 19th century context, an
odious question.*
— review of I.B. Singer's
play, *Teibele and Her Demon.*

The demon lover withdrew.
His phallus was still hard
and covered with her blood.

"There," he said, pointing it at her.
"Suck it off. Like a vampire."

She shut off her inhibitions,
thought of Germaine Greer,
and sucked.

The blood had no taste,
no odor,
almost no texture.

Which made it seem surprisingly
clean. Perhaps it was clean.

She had learned what vampires know.

TIME BY

L'AMOUR

Etre
le premier venu.

— René Char

1.

I saw him on the street today
talking with a woman,
an unidentified woman
in front of the music store,
Binzer.

I would have known him anywhere.

He is the one I have always known.

Old love.

2.

When she was sixteen
she met a man who loved her.
When she was thirty-two
they met again.
Still not too old for first love.

3.

They rolled on the straw matting that covered the floor of his lair,
water running in the sink so no one would hear them.
They fucked themselves into a ball,
like circus acrobats,
until he came,
in her mouth,
but mostly in her long hair.

4.

You make me feel not
unwanted   but like Circe
I do not lure you

to your death but to
your life   by imagining
that I will make you

my victim
you make me

yours.

5.

You're an old man now,
your blue eyes are watery.

I am not old yet.

SEX, DEATH, AND BAD TASTE IN LONDON

TO LET
said the signs
on buildings everywhere.
I had a bladder infection
that week
so I always thought it said
TO i LET
Sure if they'd meant TOILET
they'd have said
LOO

I consulted a gynecologist about my infection.
"How'd you get this?" he asked.
"Too much sex," I said.
"Most 39-year-olds complain of not enough sex," he said.
"I'm happy for you," he leered.
I was glad my friend Julia was close by.
"Give it a rest while you're in London," he advised.

At dinner I sat next to a man who told me
he was a world-class expert on pain.
"Do you give it or receive it?" I asked.
"Do you vanquish it, or what?"
"I study it," he told me.

The Russian emigré pianist sitting across from me
said he was dying of cancer. He said he had bought a house
midway between a crematorium and a Jewish cemetery.
So he would have a choice.

Yolanda said her brother in New York was an expert on AIDS.
Julia told Yolanda she complained too much about her own
ailments. Yolanda said, "You don't understand. I'm Jewish,
not English. Jewish people complain."

I told all my English friends about an article
I had read in the *International Herald Tribune*.
It said that bands of eunuchs roam India
looking for boys born without penises.
They kidnap these boys in order to perpetuate
themselves.

Julia said I was the Queen of Bad Taste.

All the men who desired me that week were married.

I gave it a rest.

III

UPSTAIRS, DOWNSTAIRS

She lived in the cellar.
It was illegal.
There was a bathroom
but no kitchen,
but that's not why it was illegal.
It was illegal because, technically,
it wasn't a basement. It was a cellar,
so called because the ceiling was a certain height,
which, according to the law, was too low
for human occupancy. It wasn't *that* low.
The son of the traveling saleswoman
who had owned the house before me
had lived there too. He was an actor
who received a lot of pornographic mail
at that address even after he moved.
And the houseman Peter, whom you met in my poem "Ghosts,"
he lived there. He was shot,
but that was after he left the premises.

So she lived in the cellar and it was illegal.
She had a bathroom but no kitchen.
She had a private entrance,
and she had a refrigerator and a hot plate.
It was a large space, but with a very low ceiling
and rent to match. I charged her very little
and we became friends.

It was good space and she made the most of it.
Peter had intended to install a Hawaiian waterfall
in the corner so it's a good thing he left when he did.
I mean before he installed the waterfall,
and before his death by accidental shooting.

He left because he and my husband couldn't get along
after the baby was born.
Then my husband left.
That was because he and I didn't get along
after our baby was born.
Maybe he couldn't get along at all.
Then Dinah came.

❖

We did get along.
I suppose if I had known
my husband was going to leave,
Peter could have stayed.
But they both left, as it were,
and Dinah came to live in the basement
apartment. She stayed a long time,
until she went to live with Arnie.

We lived like college roommates, actually.
I'd go down to see her
through the connecting door
from the house to the basement,
or she'd come up   We'd visit back and forth
at all hours, after dates and so on,
since we were both single then.
And when I came back up or she went back down
I'd slide the bolt on the cellar door,
because a burglar had come in that way
once, before she lived there,
and before Peter too   way back when
we were renovating the house,
bringing it back from the rooming-house
that the traveling saleswoman and her son
the actor had converted it into.

The burglar came in while my former husband
and I were dining with a painter,
Adja Yunkers, in the kitchen.
I heard noises and I said what's that,
and neither of them heard it
so they said oh Anne-Marie
you're always hearing things.
Which is true. I have a reputation.
But the next morning
all the portable appliances in the kitchen
were gone. The burglar had been waiting
on the cellar steps (the door having been left ajar)
for us to leave, and when we went upstairs to bed
he just came and took what he wanted.
After that I always kept the cellar door bolted.
And one day David, who was about six years old,
said Mommy, why do you always lock Dinah up
down there? He thought she was imprisoned.

She had a boyfriend named Kent,
and when he left he went with a girl
she called Miss Neatsy-Keen-New-And-Fresh.
When I think about Dinah in those days
I realize that she was, whenever possible,
naked. I remember many conversations
where she lay naked in the bath,
and I sat fully dressed on the toilet seat
talking to her in her bathroom.

If only I'd been Bonnard   Bonnard's wife
you know, spent a lot of time in the tub,
and he painted her there over and over,

indolent, self-indulgent, sensual.
They were obsessed, the Bonnards, Mr. and Mrs. —
he with her, she with bathing.
If *Kent* had been more like Bonnard!
He might not have left.

We had three-way conversations as well,
Kent and Dinah and I. We would visit sometimes
in the bedroom area of her apartment,
one of us on the bed, the others in chairs.
She would be naked, we would be dressed.

That scene has a painterly quality too,
but not like Bonnard: a naked woman
in a bedroom with an older clothed woman,
and a man, also clothed.
Very precise and mysterious.
A sense of something about to happen.
What does it suggest?
Genre painting?
The Procuress.
What does that make me?
The landlady as Madam.
It seemed perfectly natural at the time,
she was just more comfortable naked.
Her next boyfriend didn't like it though,
Arnie. And she left to go live with him.
No wonder it didn't work out.
We should have known, nudity was key.
Kent left too, of course,
but I don't think that was the reason.
I'll bet Miss Neatsy-Keen kept her clothes on though.

❖

Dinah also had what were known
as Platonic relationships.
We needed phrases like that in those days,
now we don't.
She was a generous person and any man
or woman who needed a place to stay
could share her double bed.
People were always sleeping over,
and it was perfectly okay to share a bed with a guy
and not have sex.
But one day a guy named Jerry said "Dinah,
even friends get erections."

She had nice friends.
Some of them became my friends, like Bella,
who says her son was conceived in that bed.
Dinah wanted to share Kent with me,
but he and I agreed
it would not be a good idea.
She did unwittingly share one of her friend's
boyfriends with me, but that was a dark moment,
and she wasn't nice about it.

But then she left
and went to live with Arnie in a loft.
And after his cat died
Bill came to use the place for a studio.
After his cat died?
Don't ask.
Bill's still here though, and that's good,
because it's not as though good things happened
to people after they left my house.
Rothko spent some nights here and he committed suicide.

Peter was shot.
My former husband died of cancer
and that was after he left
and after he remarried.
Dinah had a *"crise de nerfs"* (I prefer that phrase
to ours — a crisis has more imaginative
possibilities than a breakdown)
and that was after she left my house
to go live with Arnie.

So that's why I wonder —
about all the people who're gone, what it means,
and about the ones who're left. Bill's still here,
as I said, and Mo and David. And that's good.
Because it's not as though good happens
when people leave.

HOUSEHOLD TANKA

You threw a wineglass
across the kitchen at me.
It hit the wall. Our
baby in his highchair watched.
Eleven wineglasses now.

FIRST WIFE

He asked me so I said I would
He asked would I go through his dying with him
and I said yes, I said yes because what else could I say,
How could I say no

Afterwards I woke up crying every night
in the middle of the night and Bill,
Bill would hold me, wordlessly,
he never spoke there were never any words,
but I was crying for the parents,
I was imagining their grief and I took on their grief
and I thought I cried only for them

He asked would I go through it with him and I said yes
For me it was not so bad it was terrible
I lived through his death as my own so I knew
what it was I knew it long before it would happen
to me I was only forty   I figured now I knew

He called once would I come
and I went to the hospital and in the elevator
I met his wife and Why don't you go home she said
and I said I would go once he knew that I had come
When we met in his room he played us off
one against the other, not the least bit embarrassed
He was tickled silly to have us both there

When he died he was out of his mind, he was drugged
he was not unhappy   He was listening to Mozart,
the violin/piano sonatas played by Szymon Goldberg
and Lili Kraus, and he was pointing to a square of
paranoia on a spot opposite the bed, a spot where two walls met

It scared me to see him that way so I cried
but my crying scared the others so I left
If he had been clear-headed I could have stayed longer

He asked me to go there with him and I said yes
If he had been clear-headed I could have gone farther
I went as far as I could

AT DINNER

My father ate an avocado half with his dinner every night.
He carved a face into the pit every other night.
Why did he do that, I wonder now?

There were three of us at dinner every night
and Gaby who served. The vegetable man, Pete,
who was Greek, would come by the house twice a week
in his truck, and Gaby would go out and chat
and choose avocados.

Vegetables were plentiful and fruit too,
in Beverly Hills, Southern California,
the 1950s, and they were not seasonal.
We had them, and the flowers, year 'round.

We had come from Belgium, all of us.
We had fled in the first days of the War.
In those winters you had only endive and cauliflower.
Avocado every day was an abundance.

I could feel his glee as he carved.

WHO HAS THE RIGHT TO COMPLAIN? Claire

My aunt Claire told the story at dinner:
she and my mother had found themselves
with their old friend Max at a railway station
somewhere in Europe, sometime after the war.
Max's bags had somehow landed
on the German side of the railway station.

The three of them had escaped the Holocaust in Europe.
They all spoke many languages,
they all did in those days.
Max wanted his bags back, of course,
but he didn't want to go over to the German side
to get them. He didn't want to speak German either.
So he asked my mother and my aunt
to go over there for him.
Typical Max, I said.

Oh no, said Claire, you don't understand.
His grandparents committed suicide in Germany
rather than leave.
And what about your grandparents? I asked.
It's not the same, Claire said.
Our grandmother died immediately after
they took her to the concentration camp.
She died a natural death.
That's not the same? I said.
No, she said.

So she and my mother went over to the German side
and my mother didn't want to speak German either,
but she couldn't get the bags out in any other language,
so finally she did speak German and she did get them out.
Well, I said, it seems to me that you and my mother
have as much reason for not wanting to go over there
and do all that as Max did.
No! she shouted. You're wrong! And what's more —
you have very bad values.

WHO HAS THE RIGHT TO COMPLAIN? Grete

I got a ride uptown last night
from Christina's friend Grete
after Sander Gilman's lecture and dinner
with Christina at Les Halles.
Gilman lectured on the history of reconstructive
surgery to make yourself more beautiful
less noticeable or less Jewish.
Grete, who's German and not Jewish and who writes
about the Holocaust in English,
had been giving a reading of Holocaust poetry
with some other women, all Jewish.
Grete said she had been thinking about what
was wrong with the other women's poems,
and had decided that the problem was
their poems didn't have enough grit.
Christina, who's also German and not Jewish
but doesn't write about it, said what's grit?
Grete said the real pain you know?
Those women tried to pretty it up with metaphor
but there's nothing pretty about the Holocaust,
nothing pretty at all. Then she said she thought
it was almost as though they were trying to find
something good to say. I said maybe they were.

I happen to know her writing
which collects Jewish people's stories
and turns them into what I'm going to call prosettes,
little skimpy tales written largely without metaphor,
as you might imagine.
She includes stories about her own childhood
in Germany during and after the war,
with lots of complaining,
which is what, in her prosettes,
she castigates the German people for.

Why does she do all this?
Tell Jewish people's stories I mean.
Well, I figure she can't present her own
terrible childhood as anyone else could,
because she's a child of Nazis,
and people would say how can you,
how do you have the nerve to complain
when Jewish children suffered so much more
at the hands of your own people.
So she appropriates our stories.

Who are these poets? I asked.
Oh a Two G, she said, and someone born
in a displaced person's camp. (She didn't say DP)
What's a Two G? I asked.
Second Generation, she said. That's what they call them.
(Child of a Holocaust survivor. That's what the Two G means).
But their names, I asked, what are their names?

Meanwhile she's driving up Park Avenue South
like a demented person,
never braking till she hits a crosswalk,
even if it holds a pedestrian.
Christina's waving her arms and yelling The
pedestrian! the pedestrian! every few minutes.
In the midst of all this Grete turns to me
and says, And what do you do?
Oh, and what are your poems about?

All I can think of to say is they're not about the Holocaust.

poems

1.

Being very cruel
he felt he was pure,
for he was cruel
to himself
as well.

2.

Speeding boats
violate the waters.

They slice the gentle surface,
plunder the parted waves.

3.

Weak, wanting, unknowing and
unknown, she follows . . .

4.

I care about you,
but I reserve the right to
hurt you, revenge my-
self, take from you, please believe
my continuing concern.

5.

Memory matters
less than the mastery of
metaphysical
metaphors which transmit the
music   if one remembers.

WITH SOPHIE

The Sophie I knew
heard that I like snails.
So she bought a bunch at the Star Market
or she caught them in the garden
I'm not sure which,
she didn't get them from one of those French cans,
I know that.
And I thought she cooked them in brine for three days
but that's not how you do it,
it's much more complicated.
She must have washed them several times
to clean the dirt from the shells,
removed the diaphragm with the point of a small knife,
and soaked the snails in vinegar, flour, and rock salt.
She would have soaked them for two hours
to make them disgorge their viscous slime.
Then she would have washed them again in running water
to remove all the mucous substances from the shells,
and brought them to a boil very slowly,
carefully lifting the scum
produced by the remainder of the mucous substances.
Then she must have boiled them eight more minutes,
drained and cooled them, and covered them
with equal parts of white wine and water;
thick rings of carrots and onions,
sliced shallots, cloves of garlic,
a *bouquet garni* and a few peppercorns.
She would have cooked them at a slow boil
for three hours or so, and when the snails were cooked,
she would have removed them from their shells
and immediately cut off the cloaca,

the black end of the helix.
Then you're supposed to wash the shells
in warm water, drain them, and set them on a rack to dry.
But she probably didn't do that
because she served us each a bunch of snails
on a plain white plate, a dinner plate,
and she laid them out before us without the ritual,
no shells or indented dishes,
no special utensils, snail forks or holders.
A shocking sight, those bare-chested snails,
a real surprise, no, a confrontation.
"You want snails?" she seemed to be saying,
"Here are snails."

I'm telling you because I'm upset.
The announcement upset me, the announcement of her death,
coming as it did in the mail,
looking like the announcement of a marriage
or a birth, not an invitation to a memorial service
at Our Lady of the Signs Russian Orthodox Cathedral
on Ninety-third Street, that's where it was,
in the church with the divided staircase
and the choirs, male choirs with bass voices
that sound like an ocean, like waves,
the same choirs that sang for George Balanchine
when he died.
That was her heritage, antiphonal choirs,
Sophie Dobzhansky, daughter of Theodosius,
and in the invitation it was combined with her husband's:
"Reception at the Knickerbocker Club," it said,
that's what Mike's invitation said.

❖

The Sophie I knew
roasted a suckling pig for us once,
stuffed it with breadcrumbs and parsley of course,
shallots and garlic,
the grated peel of a lemon and an orange
and the juices of both.
Well-beaten eggs, pepper and nutmeg too.
There was some special occasion and she invited us
but I couldn't eat the animal.
There were about two inches of fat
under the crisp browned skin
and I couldn't eat it.
When I was little I couldn't swallow fat,
I would have vomited. Now that I'm grown
I can eat fat if I have to but not two inches.
I kept cutting small pieces and hiding them
under the mashed potatoes.
The pig had an apple in its mouth and it looked great
if you like that sort of thing, which I don't
(I'm not crazy about snails without the shells either)
but Sophie tried everything once.
I'm sure there was nothing edible she had not cooked.
She had a vegetable garden
and an edible-flower garden,
and the last book she published
was an Aztec cookbook.

❖

I'm telling you because I'm upset.
First Jackie and then Sophie.
You know how everyone remembers where they were
when John F. Kennedy was shot.
Well, I was with Sophie in New Haven.
We spent a few days together while our husbands
attended a conference, something about archaeology.
I don't remember what we did
(we must have played with the kids)
except that I read *Fanny Hill.*
Every night I'd go to bed and turn myself on
reading *Fanny Hill.*
It was my first erotic novel,
the first one it was legal to read,
and the first I'd ever read.
My first dirty book and my first assassination.
With Sophie in New Haven.

❖

The Sophie I knew
said ho-hum when she was bored
but she wasn't bored that week.
I'm telling you because I'm upset.
I don't want her gone,
I don't want Mike to be alone,

I don't want my memories to float.
Sophie! Send me a postcard,
say ho-hum for me.
Call and invite me to visit.

IV

Claustrophobia   is

the curse   of

white rats   and

mice   how

                      ever they don't know

                      that theirs is the glass

                      tribunal in which doctors

                      and medicine men

                      play their cards

luck

*The old tension, initiated by Picasso and Braque, between public
words and private sensibility has gone slack; and all private
experience can be expressed now only in the homogenized
language of a public information.*

— MOMA catalogue for "High and Low" exhibit

1.

A woman from Fresno,
infected by the AIDS virus,
was shunned by the people in her drug treatment program.
Deciding that there was no point in fighting her addiction
since she was going to die anyway,
she dropped out of the program.
Health officials found her on the street soliciting truck drivers.
She was taking no sexual precautions, she said,
nor was she cleaning her needles.
She pleaded guilty to prostitution,
entered and left another drug treatment program,
and is now in jail for violating probation.
She will be out soon,
doing the same things,
passing the AIDS virus around.
Health officials are concerned.

2.

A man named Asher Edelman,
an expert on company takeovers,
was hired by the Columbia University Business School
to teach a class in corporate raiding.
Mr. Edelman offered a finder's fee, $100,000,
to any student who could identify a company
for Mr. Edelman to raid.

The university forced Mr. Edelman to rescind the offer,
saying direct economic incentives were inappropriate
in an academic environment.
Mr. Edelman commented, "What bothers me most
is that this is a violation of the integrity
of the classroom,
of my right to teach,
and of the students' right to learn."   l(earn)?

3.

In 1963 a fishing boat crew observed
that the sea had begun to boil
south of Iceland. Subsequent eruptions
built the isle of Surtsey.

4.

Yves Volel, who was my son's math teacher
at the Dalton School in New York,
was shot to death this morning
in front of police headquarters in Port au Prince, Haiti.
He was delivering a speech
demanding the release of a prisoner.
Yves Volel was one of thirty presidential candidates,
and the second political leader to be assassinated in Haiti
in the last three months.
In a telephone interview with the Dalton School newspaper
shortly after resigning from the school to return to Haiti
Mr. Volel had said, "If I have to die,
I will die."

5.

President Reagan has vowed
that his next appointment to the Supreme Court,
if Judge Bork is defeated,
will be as upsetting to his foes
as Bork's appointment was.
"If I have to appoint another judge,"
said the President,
"I'll try to find one that they'll object to
just as much as they did to this one."

6.

Somewhere in the South Central Pacific
an undersea volcano has erupted,
and this volcano has erupted directly beneath
a research ship from California.
A great noise was heard
and the ship rattled and shook,
and as it rattled and shook huge bubbles of steam and gas
burst under its hull and in the water around it.
One gigantic bubble rose six feet above the ocean surface
and then exploded,
shooting out jets of gas and exposing in its core
a cluster of twenty or thirty volcanic rocks.
The rocks were so filled with gas that, briefly,
they floated.

MORTISE AND TENON

Note: In carpentry

Waiting,

a tenon is a projecting part

> *the scent of her creature*
> *fills the room*

cut on the end of a piece of wood

> *inside her granny nightgown*

for insertion into a corresponding hole

> *She inhales deeply, deeply*
> *drawn to the pursuit of her nature*

(mortise) in another piece of wood

> *A flash of arrogant body, and his ebullient sex*
> *jumps the flannel barrier . . .*

to fasten securely.

> *Finding her at home, he binds himself to her.*
> *The room is no longer hers*

To joint by mortise and tenon.

SCHNABEL 0, HUROK 1

How pleasant
to be sitting musing in my bedroom,
to feel a poem begin its journey
from inwardness to lucidity   Schnabel

to cross the hall to the room where I write
thinking how quiet I was,
how excited I will be . . .

    The telephone rings in the bedroom
He is calling to tell me the call he is awaiting
has not yet come . . .

If it doesn't want to come you can't stop it   Hurok

How pleasant it was.

ELLSWORTH KELLY —

the primacy of man's need
for color, the poignancy
of man's need
for primary color

TIME OUT

Saturday afternoon we went straight to Malibu
from the airport and had a snack on Richard's terrace
overlooking the ocean.
I got some sun on my face, it was great,
we felt good. Lisa came to dinner and was voluble
and pleased at being at the beach, we drank a bottle
of Pouilly Fuissé 1987, Louis Jadot,
and Flora said it was the best bottle of wine
she had ever tasted . . .

My friend Chris Wilmarth
the sculptor
hanged himself yesterday in his studio
in Brooklyn . . .
He was forty-four
and being treated for depression

Anyway, as I said, we felt great on the terrace
in the sun at Malibu.
By now it was Sunday and we were free,
we couldn't visit Celia because she had fallen and broken
her hip the day before, we didn't know, we were in the air,
and we couldn't go to the poster auction
because Bill had left the address in New York and the tickets too,
so we were free.
Non-stop talker Helen was expected to descend
for the afternoon though, so to defend ourselves
we went to the tiny Malibu shopping mall
and turned up a fabulous denim jacket
called distressed,

and a crimson hat,
perfect for protecting my hair in the sun,
you can even lie on it.
It's big enough for my head too,
I have a very big head.
Ten dollars.

When we got back to Richard's
I called New York and I found out that Betty had died.
So I called Rachel and she said that Vladimir had told her
that Betty had been having nightmarish morphine hallucinations
and that the last one before she died had been about me.
Spooked me . . . I really wanted to know *what* she had hallucinated
about me but I couldn't very well call Vladimir, who was Betty's
husband, and say, hey, by the way . . .

I read in the *L.A. Times*, by the way,
that according to the Asthma and Allergy Foundation
of America, 40% of the weed pollens in the air
over here are from hemp. That's marijuana.
People here are having allergy attacks
from marijuana pollen.

My friend Maggie is having a nervous breakdown
back in New York,
they call it severe depression
with alcohol dependency.
I was upset about that.
She sits around and cries and drinks
and is getting thinner and thinner and
the last thing she said to me before we left
— she wants my life.

Sunday evening
we went to a new Southwest-style restaurant
called Malibu Adobe,
created by movie stars who live in Malibu
because, as they say,
there are no good restaurants there.
I ate the black bean soup
and had diarrhea all the next day,
and that day was Monday,
the day we drove to Palm Springs.

Monday's *L.A. Times* had an article
which said that Beverly Hills qualifies for Federal aid
under the Distressed Cities program,
but it is not planning to exercise its option to apply.
Another small California city, Maywood, inhabited by aging
Latinos, was excluded from the list, which is published
by the U.S. Department of Housing and Urban Affairs.
Beverly Hills has been on the list for several years.

So we arrived in Palm Springs
and I wasn't feeling too great
what with the upset stomach and all,
and I even thought I detected a sore throat,
but it was only the effect of the dryness
created by the fabulous air-conditioner
of our rented Chrysler New Yorker which was
great too except for the computer-generated male voice
which keeps telling you your "sheat belts"
are not "fashened" and your washer fluid is low.
So I headed for the backyard Jacuzzi we had requested

but the water was tepid and the bubbles were low. We uncorked
the Pouilly Fumé Ladoucette I had brought and it was vinegar.
So I got into the bathtub saying what else can go wrong.
Five minutes later the water was sloshing around
in the tub, the doors were swinging back and forth
and I had vertigo. If I'd been in the Jacuzzi
I might not have noticed, but either a truck
has just driven into the side of the house or
it's an earthquake, I said. Sure enough
it was a six point something on the Richter scale.
We had driven to Palm Springs just in time
to experience one of the worst rumbles in recent history,
only 80 miles from the epicenter. It was fun though,
and I learned a lot. A bad earthquake, as Darwin said,
destroys our oldest associations. The earth,
the very emblem of solidity, moves beneath our feet
like a thin crust over a fluid. It's true.
And something else: the earth doesn't quake
in an earthquake. It jiggles.

FOUR NOVEMBER 9THS

My family expected I would be born on Armistice Day,
November 11, and that would be one thing,
that would have been something to joke about
in those days. But I came into being two days earlier,
on November 9, in the evening, and that was another thing,
it was not a joke, and it was evidently not a thing
to be remembered or told,
because I was not made aware of the coincidence
of my birth until several months before my 50th birthday,
which coincided with, and was commemorated and announced as,
the 50th anniversary of Kristallnacht.
So there I was, and even more than that here I am,
quite surprised, not to mention still unprepared,
and quite unable to avoid thinking about both at once.
The reminders since then have been constant and grim.
Coincidence: the visible traces of invisible principles.

And now my friend Gottfried Wagner,
who since the day he discovered the date
has never forgotten my birthday,
has informed me that there are four November 9ths
in history, that it is a very big day in the history of Germany
in this century. There is even a book written,
it is called *The Four November 9ths*.
I can't read the book, it is written in German,
but I have done some research, and as far as I can tell

The first November 9 was 1918;
it was a revolution in which the Kaiser abdicated,
which culminated in the Proclamation of the Republic in Berlin
on November 9. The above-mentioned Armistice
between the Allies and Germany
followed on the 11th.

The second November 9 was 1923;
it was Hitler's abortive "Beer Hall Putsch"
against the Bavarian government in Munich.
Hitler, who was at first imprisoned, eventually emerged
as the undisputed leader of the radical right.

The third November 9 was, as you know, My November 9th,
Kristallnacht.

And on November 9, 1989, the Berlin Wall came down.

So there you are and here we are, on my birthday,
and all of this is to say what Gertrude Stein has already said,
what can I teach you about history — history teaches.

It is not a simple matter, the birthday, or the telling.

AUTHOR'S NOTES

In "Night's Bodies" I quote myself.

The quotes in "Dreams, Fragments" are from Beckett, Freud, and Jabès.

In "Tunnel Vision," the quote is from Milton's *Paradise Lost*.

The last line in "Mournful Nutrients" is by Mies van der Rohe.

The review in "On Being Clean" is by Brendan Gill.

"With Sophie": *Fanny Hill Or, Memoirs of a Woman of Pleasure* was written by John Cleland in 1749.

I rephrase Gertrude Stein in "Four November 9ths." The actual lines read, "Let me repeat what history teaches. History teaches."

ANNE-MARIE LEVINE was born in Belgium and raised in Beverly Hills. She's a poet and scholar who began to write while touring as a concert pianist. A board member at Poets House, she's the author of a prize-winning book of poems called *Euphorbia*, and the recipient of a NYFA grant for poetry. She also performs solo theater pieces based on her poems. She has published essays on Gertrude Stein's politics, and on art and trauma, and has received grants from the Puffin and Vogelstein Foundations for this work. Her current projects include a Commonplace Book, and an exhibit of visual art called *Boxpoems*.